53 Poems By God and I

Volume I

by
Darcy A. Venables

Bloomington, IN

Milton Keynes, UK

AuthorHouse™
1663 Liberty Drive, Suite 200
Bloomington, IN 47403
www.authorhouse.com
Phone: 1-800-839-8640

AuthorHouse™ UK Ltd.
500 Avebury Boulevard
Central Milton Keynes, MK9 2BE
www.authorhouse.co.uk
Phone: 08001974150

First published by AuthorHouse 2/19/2007

ISBN: 978-1-4259-9142-5 (sc)

Library of Congress Control Number: 2007900346

Printed in the United States of America
Bloomington, Indiana

This book is printed on acid-free paper.

"If you knew Who walks beside you on the way that you have chosen, fear would be impossible"

"Be tempted not to snatch away the gift of faith you offered to your brother. You will succeed only in frightening yourself. The gift is given forever, for God Himself received it. You can not take it back. You have accepted God." (Quotes from A Course in Miracles)

Light and Love and Special thanks too;
Our Editor and Loving friend, Maggy Davidson
My Best friend, Helga Venables
And GOD, (and not necessarily in this order)

Darcy Venables

VOLUME ONE
INTRODUCTION

Dear friends,

If you need a word to help you
He will give it to you
If you need a thought
This will also be given to you
If you need stillness and peace
These are gifts you will also receive
When He is in charge by your request
He will hear and answer you
Because you know you are not alone.

Thank you God.

CONTENTS

I Am Beside You

I'm at the crossroads on this path
Father show me the way to go
I need to know which way to turn
Father I know you know

I'm asking for Your guidance
I'm searching for Your light
Father please shine upon
The path the one that's right

I can not do this all alone
Father please don't let me stray
If You just walk beside me
I know I'll find the way

But son I am beside you
I know you've always known
Wherever I am you are
You could never be alone.

A FEATHER ON THE FLOOR

An Angel picked me up today
One I've never seen
We're going for a ride She said
To a place you've never been

Her steady wings wrapped around
And cradled me with ease
So soft and fresh without a sound
I felt their gentle breeze

Then up we went and soared away
And She whispered in my ear
There's a door that I must show you
It's very close to here

And suddenly there it was
A door that's pure white
A door that emanates with love
This door is made of light

Her graceful wings set me down
The brightness was too much
With extended hands I closed my eyes
And felt its loving touch

And at that moment I awoke
And sat up in my bed
Was I just at the door of light
These thoughts ran through my head

Did I just dream this Angel
Did I just dream this door
And as I looked around my room
I found a feather on the floor.

A PLACE CALLED HEAVEN

Wild flowers paint the hills
A rainbow in the sky
Water falling in a mist
And a blue bird passing by

Ripples dance across a pond
Dewdrops clinging too a tree
An apple tree in blossoms
So pleasing too a bee

The refreshing sent of pine trees
Wild mushrooms here and there
A bed of moss so green and soft
A cub and a mother bear

Snow capped Rocky Mountains
A lake that sparkles green
A sun that shines on everything
And a fawn that goes unseen

Who said we had to pass away
Who said we had to go
To find a place called Heaven
We're in it don't you know.

A WOODEN HORSE

Castle's, knights and a wooden horse
A magic world for a child of course
A wooden sword and a mop for a spear
You fend them off as they draw near

And as you meet those knights in black
You know you'll win when they attack
You're a knight in white and their to fight
All those who come within your sight

You have no fear, no second thought
Just into battle, horse at a trot
Out in the back then onto the lawn
You fight them all till the day is gone

You're by yourself, you're all alone
The only one to protect the throne
And it's all so real, it's all just there
And the battles go by without a care

Now is it magic or is it true
At four years old each day is new
So why does it change as we grow old
Why can't we stay with those knights so bold

From a world of magic to a place unkind
Why do we leave this child behind?

I am a Lighthouse

I am a lighthouse and the light
A glowing shine that floods the night

I am a rock that's always there
I hold the lighthouse firm with care

I am the ocean water deep
I clean the rock I never sleep

I am the breeze that sooths the rock
Come listen close and I will talk

I am a ship that passes near
I feel the light I have no fear

I am the mist, an ocean spray
A cleansing feeling for this day

I am a dove that sores above
I guard them all I share their love

I am a lighthouse and the light
Together we shine so clear and bright.

I am His son

I am His son
He walks with me
And with each step
I am set free

I am His son
He's part of me
It is His sight
With which I see

I am His son
His thoughts are mine
And with His thoughts
I am Divine

I am His son
His voice I hear
I feel His strength
I have no fear

I am His son
He is the way
And on His path
I can not stray

I am His son
His love I hold
He walks with me
His path is gold.

WHERE HAVE ALL THE DRAGONS GONE.

Where have all the dragons gone
Does anybody know
They use to play from dusk to dawn
And put on quite a show

On misty days you'd hear them roar
Their sight was never keen
But in the sun they'd play some more
Their games were never mean

Up and down, then to and fro
They'd frolic in the sky
Then a puff of smoke would let us know
That they just said goodbye

And in the morning there they'd be
As we looked on from the shore
Then a flame or two made sure we'd see
And watch them play some more

Now with all there power and all their might
And flames that they can through
I never seen the dragons fight
As play is all they know

So where did all the dragons go
They vanished overnight
Their time on earth was just to show
To play is not to fight.

THREE WISHES

If I had three wishes
I'd give them all away
Perhaps I'd give them all to you
Just to brighten up your day

If I had three wishes
Perhaps I might just say
Is there anybody out there
Who needs a wish today

If I had three wishes
Perhaps I'd split them up
Give one to you, and one to you
And one to you with the empty cup

If I had three wishes
And you were passing by
I'd use one wish to wish you in
To see that sparkle in your eye

But if I only had one wish
I'd wish for you to stay
Because whenever you're around
I seem to have a perfect day.

WALK THE WALK

It's not too hard to talk the talk
The words come out and they may be true
But to let it all go and walk the walk
Is the hardest thing you'll ever do

With every moment in each day
To walk in light and know it's true
To keep his faith and to know His way
Is the hardest thing you'll ever do

Having total trust in what you know
And shedding things you thought you knew
And to let Him guide the way to go
Is the hardest thing you'll ever do

But once you know you'll never stray
You know his way is true
You're in His light and there to stay
It's now the easiest thing that you will do.

SURRENDER

Surrender just let it go
You think you're in control
Give the steering wheel back to God
And peace will fill your soul

Sit back and buckle up
You'll find this quite a ride
When you no longer have to steer
It's relief you'll feel inside

The road ahead I know
Is a path you never knew
But God is back in the driver's seat
So you know for sure it's true

So look around enjoy the ride
I know you'll like the view
With God back in control
This world you'll find is new

We all think that we're the ones
We think we're in control
But give the steering wheel back to God
And lighten up your soul.

WITHIN

There are two worlds that we live in
One is without and one is within
It is a choice it's up to you
Between what you know and what is true

But it can be sad to live without
There may be pain there will be doubt
There's heavy weight to pack around
It can't be seen and has no sound

But the burden is there it's nothing new
And it is your choice it's up to you.

Now to live within and to feel the light
Just to know it's there all within your sight
Will lift the weight from the world without
It removes the pain and sheds the doubt

And you find a peace that will overtake
Any feeling of hurt, any feeling of hate
And to stay within is like a high
It will lift you up, you will learn to fly

So pick the world you'd like to be in
You can live without or you can choose within.

HAVE YOU EVER SEEN

Have you ever watched a butterfly
As it flutters here and there
Or seen an osprey in the sky
Diving through the air

Have you glanced around and seen a fawn
Hidden on the ground
Or seen some deer at early dawn
Moving without a sound

Have you seen a squirrel up in a tree
Building its winter bed
Or a flock of geese in a perfect V
Flying over head

Have you ever seen a wild horse
Running like it's free
Or an elephant with all its force
Uprooting a giant tree

Have you ever seen an eagle's nest
With young ones being fed
Or seen a quail with his little crest
Bobbing on his head

Have you seen the great blue heron stand
With one leg tucked away
Or watched a tortoise cross the sand
In the heat of a sunny day

Do you wonder what it's all about
Like a lion when he roars
I'd have to say without a doubt
It's God as he plays outdoors.

A DREAM

I woke the other day to say
This dream I have won't go away

I have it every night you see
It's all about just being free

Free to fly all through the sky
And fly I do without a try

I've had this dream since I was small
But in my dream I'm very tall

And I can do most anything
I dance, I play, I even sing

It's peace this dream instills in me
My dream that always sets me free

So tell me how to keep so free
When I'm awake and life I see.

WHAT IS REAL?

A sky so blue
And trees so green
Can this be true
What I have seen

This world we see
And things we feel
Can this all be
Can this be real

To touch the ground
Or to smell a flower
Just to hear a sound
Emanates with power

This power we share
Like the radiant sun
And together with care
We feel as one

So be kind too all
No matter its size
From mountains so tall
To the little fruit flies.

An Angels wings

There are some things
That go untold
About Angels wings
As they unfold

To feel their breeze
The freshness of
And with such ease
Out flows their love

They open wide
In silent peace
You feel inside
Your heart increase

They wrap around
And embrace your soul
Without a sound
You loose control

Their golden light
Fills up your spine
A shine so bright
You feel divine

The feeling's bliss
This gentle hold
As an Angels kiss
Is never cold

There are some things
That go untold
About Angels wings
As they unfold.

THE LITTLE ONE INSIDE

To see your little one inside
Brings feeling you can never hide

To embrace this little one we see
Is to drift as high as you can be

To keep this little one so near
Is to shed your total life of fear

To feel the fragrance of its youth
Is to live a life in total truth

To hold its little hand so fair
Is to walk in life with loving care

To love this little one within
Is to cleanse your total life of sin

So guard this little one you keep
When you're awake or as you sleep.

A RAINBOW

I glanced across the lake to see
A rainbow in the sky
A little gift from God for me
So pleasing to the eye

I had to stop, I had to stare
I felt it from within
I couldn't move, I didn't dare
To leave would be a sin

With colors crisp and very bold
It stretched across the earth
The beauty felt can not be told
The feeling held it's worth

As it slowly moved across the sky
It's colors held so bright
I felt a tear drop from my eye
And I thanked God for this sight

For God to share with us this sight
This archway from above
He's telling us that it's alright
For all to share His love.

A SONG I KNOW

There is a little song I know
I sing it to myself
The places it just lets me go
Fills my heart with wealth

The words are always new you see
They flow out with each day
And different places I will be
Just makes me want to say

The beauty that we keep inside
We must not hold it there
Just let it out don't let it hide
Your love is there to share

So sing your song out loud today
Just share it with the air
And see who comes along too say
I see you really care.

When I was just a little boy

Buried deep within my mind
Hiding there and so unkind
Haunting me for oh so long
It had me thinking I'd been wrong

And pain it's caused me all that while
Had put my mind into denial
And hid these evil thoughts from me
But now I know and I am free

When I was just a little boy
I was handled like a toy
Those folks I was entrusted in
Did things to me and all in sin

I forgive myself for believing
I kept a child within that was grieving
I am lighter now for knowing this
And the light within is truly bliss.

IS THERE ANY BUDDY THERE

A gentle brush across my face
From a sudden gust of air.
Then, gone without a trace
Is there any buddy there

A chill runs up and down my spine
And a quiver in my heart.
The sensation left is so divine
These thoughts begin to start

What touches with such gentleness
Who seems to pass so near
What is this feeling in the air
This feeling that's so clear

I know I'm not alone you see
I feel you everywhere
You seem so close, you seem to be
This loving tender care

And when I'm down or feeling bad
And thoughts just seem to stray
You seem to know this day I've had
And come and clear the way

So please don't leave me, never go
Keep pressing on my heart
This feeling always lets me know
That we are not apart.

THE LETTER

I got this letter in the post
I think the sender was a ghost

The glossy paper within read
Thoughts that came from in my head

And as I thought, the words appeared
I'm telling you it's really weird

The more I thought, the more they came
Who sent this trick, this silly game

If thoughts were good, good words were there
This letter didn't seem to care

If I thought bad, or I got mad
The words just leaped onto the pad

And as I looked at what I read
These words just popped into my head

I better watch the things I think
As life goes by within a blink.

I AM

I am earth, I am tree
I am wind, I am sea

I am plant, I am root
I am seed, I am fruit

I am star, I am night
I am day, I am light

I am all, I am one
I am soul, I am sun

I am her, I am he
I am them, I am me

I know where I'm from
And I know who I am
And I say this to you

I am, that I am.

THE GREAT BLUE HEREON

Oh please tell me gentle one
Your thoughts before this day is done

You stand so silent, straight and tall
Not a movement, not a call

Such patients for your coming prey
Your stillness seems to hold the day

You step so gentle, slow and clean
In waters below no ripples seen

The wisdom held within yourself
So stern and solemn filled with wealth

This world would be a kinder place
If we could hold your gentle pace

Oh please tell me gentle one
Your thoughts before this day is done.

LOVE YOURSELF

When I look into my mirror
What I see is oh so clear

Eyes with such a piercing glare
Telling me with loving care

Before the world can see you shine
Yourself must love you as divine

Love the one you see in there
Total love with tender care

Then and only then you'll see
What a glorious place this is to be

Total love you now can give
To each and all on earth that live

And feel the love return to you
Yourself has changed, yourself is new.

IN THE NIGHT

In the dark of the night
With a pale moon light
I rambled through the trees

And the path I tread
Cast shadows that led
My mind to thought with ease

They danced I swear
Over here, over there
Every step I took they were near

As they chilled my bones
I could feel their moans
Dark spirits without fear

Now the winds blew cold
And the sounds were bold
As I hurried on my way

With every step I took
In the dark eyes looked
They hungered for this day

The thoughts in mind
Grew very unkind
These shadows blocked all sight

Should I stop, should I hide
No, go my heart cried
Just tricks not seen in the light

It's the moon in the night
And the mind that cause fright
In the light it's a beautiful sight.

MR. CATNESS

There was a cat named Mr. Catness
He sat by the wall near a hole
And he never bothered anyone
He never bothered a soul.

There was a mouse called Mouseness
And he lived inside the wall
Where he went about his business
He was cute but kinda small

Now Mouseness had this yearning
To see what it's like to be
On the other side of the wall
Just to see what there is to see

So he changed his name to Catness
And dressed up like a cat
Then he ventured through the hole
And there Mr. Catness sat

Now Mr. Catness is not a bully
He's a very friendly guy
And now he's even smiling
As he just had Mouseness pie!

You see the cat was doing Catness
That's all he wants to do
And if the mouse had just stayed Mouseness
His life would not be through.

THREE WITCHES

There are three Witches I have seen
They gather in the night
Helga, Rosie and Christine
Together there're quite a sight

And when they are together
They always close their door
What ever it is they're doing
I've heard it shakes the floor

I know the temperature in their room
Rises on its own
What ever it is they're brewing
Why can't it all be shown

I've heard their windows rattle
If you hear a cackling sound
What kind of spells are they casting
When we are not around

I think I'm going to stay the night
I'll find out what they do
I have to find out what it is
Before this night is through

There are three Angels now I know
I found out in the night
Helga, Rosie and Christine
Are the bringers of the light.

YESTERDAYS POOP

Yesterdays poop
Has gone away
I flushed it down
It tried to stay
I do not want you
Don't you see
If you hang around
In pain I'll be

Today is here
Tomorrow is not
And yesterday's fears
Don't mean a lot
So do today
What can be done
Leave yesterday back there
And tomorrow will come.

A MAGIC WAND

I came across a black bird
She had a broken wing
I touched her with my magic wand
And she began to sing

I chanced upon a black bear
His claw was split in two
I touched him with my magic wand
It's now as good as new

I found a lonely beaver
His tooth had fallen out
I touched him with my magic wand
And he scampered all about

I met a little field mouse
A broken leg she had
I touched her with my magic wand
No more will she be sad

My magic wand is quite unique
But it's not the only one
Our Father shares his light with all
There's one for every son.

A GIFT

There is a little something
I would like to share
It's all I have to give
And I give because I care

It's the only thing I own
And of this I have a lot
So to share it is a pleasure
Without a second thought

So here it is for you
This little gift of mine
To you I give my love
Because to me you are divine.

THE REAL ME

I have to go to town today
There's something I will buy
One just like the one you have
My very own third eye

I've got to get my own because
I know there's things you see
And it has to be that eye
That lets you see the things too be

So share with me the secrets
Of your eye that doesn't sleep
When I have my eye installed
Do I start with just a peep

Now when my eye is working
And I see the things you see
With my very own third eye
Perhaps I'll see the real me.

THE MAGIC WORLD

What happened to the magic world
That place we used to go
That place where we could always hide
And no one else would know

Where is that magic world we had
As children we could stay
That magic place that was so kind
And so safe for us to play

A magic world that held no pain
And hate could not come in
Just fantasy and make-believe
And games we'd always win

I have to find that magic world
I'm going back today
This other place is so unkind
I'm going back to stay

This magic world I've left behind
This place I'm looking for
God, if you would be so kind
Please help me find the door.

Forgiveness

Forgiveness is my reason
This is why I'm here
Forgiveness is the only way
I know that God is near

Forgiveness is my path
The only road I know
Forgiveness shines its light
On this path with which I go

Forgiveness is my strength
My guide throughout the day
Forgiveness holds me steady
I know I will not stray

Forgiveness is my salvation
It's the feeling that is rite
Forgiveness is my savior
It turns darkness into light.

SOURCE

Close your eyes just for awhile
Be still without a thought
Listen for the voice of Source
There's thing that we've forgot

Be silent now, be very still
We are not alone
This voice you hear, the one within
Is the Source of all that's known

This Source of light, this Source of love
Knows everything that's been
Knows everything that will be
As nothing goes unseen

So what do you want to know
Perhaps a memory gone astray
This Source is hear to share
So just ask on any day

So take a moment of your day
Be silent, just be still
And listen for the voice of Source
The Source of all good will.

A LITTLE POEM

I got this little poem today
It came from up above
It says He's bringing us a gift
He's here to share his love

This little poem is quite unique
It's just a line or two
It doesn't take Him long you see
To do what He's here to do

This little poem is here for us
So spread it all about
This gift He brings is for us all
Not one is left without

This little poem comes to an end
But within it you can see
The only gift He gives away
Is His love for you and me.

HE HOLDS MY HAND

He walks beside me
I have no fear
How can I doubt
When He's so near

He holds my hand
He knows my heart
He has my thoughts
We can not part

With Him I'm one
He knows my name
He never leaves
We are the same

There is no moment
Within the day
That He's not with me
He can not stray

He walks beside me
He lights the way
He holds my hand
How can I stray.

A LITTLE SPARKLE

There is a little sparkle
In every child's eye
Especially in the young ones
Have you ever wondered why

When you see the children smiling
Pay attention to their eyes
They're telling us their secrets
And they're very, very wise

They're telling us they know
Many things that we've forgot
One secret they will share
Is that we've been here quite a lot

They want to tell us where they've been
Or the place where they will go
You see they're smiling for a reason
And they want us all to know

If they could only tell us
But they can't, so they must show
And this little sparkle in their eye
Is the only way they know.

LISTEN TO THE ANIMALS

I looked up on a hillside
And saw a sight quite odd
Animals just standing there
And I felt the love of God

They didn't seem to mind
That I was standing there
Their glowing eyes were saying
We're here because we care

I wasn't there to harm
And they knew it, then I knelt
When they came a little closer
This is what I felt

My heart just starting pounding
My hands began to shake
This love they seem to emanate
It is almost hard to take

Their eyes are filled with power
Their eyes are full of love
It's their only way of talking
And what they say comes from above

They're telling us a story
They've been watching all along
They're telling all the people
There's things were doing wrong

You shouldn't treat the earth this way
You shouldn't hurt the sky
We're only here to help you
So please give this a try

Try to be more loving
And treat this earth with care
Take a moment every morning
Close your eyes and see what's there

In the stillness of this moment
Can you see what's really true
Can you feel what we are saying
Do you know what we've been through.

MY STUFF

That's not my stuff
I gave it away
How come its back
On the very same day

It seems to have grown
I can feel its weight
Who brought it back
On the very same date

Its stuff I don't want
It's causing me pain
Please somebody take it
And you may need a crane

I give it away
It keeps coming back
Is this some kinda game
I'm starting to crack

If I give it to you
And you take it away
Why does it come back
It just wants to stay

Then this wise old owl
Said give it to me
Make sure its well bound
And I'll set you free.

MR. SCARLET

An pileated woodpecker
Comes to visit me
He seems to like the flavor
In this knotted up old tree

When I hear somebody knocking
Out behind the shed
I know it's Mr. Scarlet
Reds the color on his head

He'll peck away for hours
He doesn't seem to mind
Perhaps a tasty tree like this
Is kinda hard to find

He also likes a tin roof
Or the metal on a post
I think he likes to hear himself
It's himself he loves the most.

LISTEN TO THE CHILDREN

Just listen to the children
Watch them as they play
See the love they emanate
What are they trying to say

Just listen to the children
Watch their every move
They're telling us a story
They have nothing here to prove

Just listen to the children
Watch them as they walk
Listen to each footstep
There's no need for us to talk

Just listen to the children
Watch them as they dance
Watch them as they swing about
They're not just here by chance

Just listen to the children
What are they trying to say
Their kind and gentle movements say
We all must learn to play.

The moon

I watched the moon at 4 AM
So full and oh so bright
Slowly move across the sky
On a clear and star filled night

I had to sit and watch it
I watched it through the night
Its beauty and its brightness
Was such a glorious sight

It shone upon the water
Its reflection was of gold
I had this thought of Angels
Gold's their color I've been told

It slowly moved behind the pines
Its light reflecting through
It gave a haunting feeling
Can this picture all be true

This moon we see is such a sight
With its light that shines so bright
It's just Gods way of saying
I'm here all through night.

THANKFULNESS

I saw a little bluebird
And it flew so close to me
It landed in an orchard
In a wise old apple tree

It pecked away at apples
Until it had its fill
Then it started singing
As I sat so very still

Its beak was pointing upward
As it chirped its melody
I think that it was thanking
That wise old apple tree

It sang its song into the night
It couldn't seem to leave
It sang its song with such delight
This is what I believe

This song, it sings with beauty
This song, it sings with love
This song, it sings with thankfulness
The love comes from above.

DANCE

Dance, Dance
Like a shadow of
Become their shape
Become their love

They may be wolf
Or they may be bear
But do their dance
And dance with care

Dance, Dance
Become their voice
Make their sounds
Let it be your choice

But to know they're near
Both night and day
You'll have to dance
You learn to play

Dance, Dance
We all must dance
To feel their strength
To know their stance

They will protect
As you will see
But you have to dance
To learn to be free

Dance, Dance
And you will find
What they bring
Will ease your mind

So to have their strength
Or to know their will
You have to dance
And not be still.

A PART OF BEING ONE

I saw a tiny dewdrop
Just clinging to a tree
It made me kinda wonder
Is this little dewdrop me

I see a prickly pinecone
Up in a tree so tall
And as I looked I wondered
If I could be that small

I look up to the milky way
And I see a falling star
I wondered then could that be me
Could I be up so far

I see a little snowflake
Falling from the sky
I feel a part of me in it
The one I see go by

I see a passing beetle
Smartly walking by
Can I be in this little shell
I think I'd like to try

I find a shiny pebble
All weather-worn and smooth
I feel within its silence
For me it seems to soothe

The beauty and the warmth
From the power of our sun
Is something that we share each day
It's a part of being one.

THIS ONES FOR YOU

This ones for you
Please take it away
It's something I do
I give every day

For it's something I had
That I didn't require
And you looked kinda sad
Now I hope you feel higher

Don't feel obligated
To give in return
As I have just stated
I give with concern

But if you have something
You don't really require
Just give me a ring
We'll lift someone else higher.

INFINITY

There is a place, it's hard see
This place is called Infinity

It's waiting here for you and me
For you and me to be set free

It's total love, It's made of light
And everything It is, is right

There is no judge, no final call
There's only love, It loves us all

It shines upon us night and day
It never sleeps, It's there too stay

So take this shine, it's free for all
It yearns for us to make this call

Then close your eyes and clear your mind
And you will find She's oh so kind.

THE LAST TWO INDIANS

They know they're the last two Indians when
All the stars are shining and it's minus ten

The campfires rocken and they're sitting tight
As the wind keeps howling throughout the night

The crows are silent in the trees all-round
As the moons crystal shadow spreads over ground

The cat and the dog just ran to the shed
But they'd rather be in the house on the bed

The shadows from the fire dance all around
As the sparks leap higher with a crackling sound

The crispy air with the darkness of the night
And the flames from the fire make everything right

So they're not giving up and they're not going in
It's these last two Indians that stay for the win.

A poem for Verna Dankwerth

Can you find it in your heart
To think of us as not apart

I haven't gone that far away
I'm in your heart, I'm in to stay

The place I had you couldn't beat
But where I'm now is oh so sweet

I never really wanted much
Just simple things, a loving touch

No complaints, I have not one
My life was clean and so much fun

Please hug the man that stood with me
He stood there strong just like a tree

Simple ways were his and mine
Together we made a life divine

So grieve no more, just smile this way
I'm in you heart, I'm there to stay.

ILLUSION

This may create confusion
And cause a revolution
But life is an illusion
And not a constitution

You're sitting in a chair
That isn't really there
And if you really care
The chair is made of air

The people that we meet
And talk to on the street
Are really kind of sweet
Illusions, ain't it neat

Now the father of us all
Isn't sitting in some hall
Watching as we squall
Just to make a judgment call

This message I must share
Because I really care
To make you all aware
That we weren't really there

Were not really on this earth
So treat it with some worth
And let it have new berth
Let new illusions walk on earth.

So Wrong

I've been so, so wrong
So long I've been wrong
Believing this me
Was actually mine
And it was Devin
You see a donor
Came along with a loaner
I'm not the owner

Now you see this me
Had decided to see
What it's like to be
On this earth and be free
To walk like the me
That I thought was the me

Now the actual me
Is more like a we
And we can be
And have and see
As long as some donors
Comes along with the loaners
You see we're not the owners.

THE POWER OF WE

Oh my brothers don't you see
It's we, it's we, it's not just me

To save this glorious world this hour
Together as one we have the power

We see, we hear, the news, all bad
Why can't they send good news, not sad

What will it take to make us see
The world as it was meant to be

We are so many but we are one
And together we shine just like the sun

Oh my brothers a world of love
Will bring us powers from above

And a glorious light so clean and white
Will shine on you and me this night

Oh my brothers don't you see
It's we, it's we, it's not just me.

SHADOWS

Shadows moving in the night
Dark shadows in the day
What are these shadows that I see
Are we perhaps their prey

You only seem to see them
From the corner of my eye
They know if you are looking
I can't always see them when I try

I wonder who they really are
And what they're doing here
I feel a strange vibration
If they get a little near

They seem to only show
For a very certain kind
The reason why, we're not sure
Perhaps it's connected to our mind

This earth may be more crowded
Than we have ever known
Have you ever had the feeling
That perhaps we're not alone.

ADDITIONAL POEMS BY HELGA VENABLES

I am who I am

I am who I am
And this is now clear
Life is worth living
And I give myself a cheer

The leader that I am
I now know that I can
Hold my people able
Without putting onto them a label

The future is bright
The skies are clear
When I am looking for an answer
I will look into a mirror.

THERE IS A SMILE ON MY FACE

There is a smile on my face
And a sparkle in my eye
It's the excitement within me
About life on a high

Sometimes however,
the smile and sparkle seem to be gone
By my thoughts created
Like the clouds that hide the sun

After a few cloudy days
The sun reappears
It seems to be brighter
Like the smile on my face.

I am Copper Island

I am this beautiful island, the only one on this beautiful lake called Shuswap Lake. I am proud, stand erect. I am free, yet I am connected to the world.

I live in harmony with my surroundings and I give people on the lake pleasure to look at, or to walk upon me. My trails are steep and cool in the shade, steep yet hot in the sun.

Some winters when the lake freezes over I invite animals like deer to live on me, the birds and insects are plenty and make the cycle of nature complete. The one thing I like best about being an island is that every person on this lake call me "My Island", I in return send out my beauty and the thoughts of love, peace, serenity, happiness, prosperity, and health to all that can see the beauty that I am.

Born April 26 1953 in Vancouver B.C. Canada. Presently living in Sorrento B.C. on the beautiful Shuswap lake. Poems starting coming to me in the fall of 2002 as I became attuned to the actuality of this life we live on this wonderful planet. This journey I have traveled, from a miss understood childhood to an awakened state of reality has been very challenging but well worth every step. Thank you God for the experiences so far.

http://www.godandi.ca

Printed in the United States
71292LV00006B/123